A Potentially Quite Remarkable Thursday

A Potentially Quite
Remarkable Thursday

poems by

Jeff Coomer

Last Leaf PRESS

• Charlottesville, VA •

Charlottesville, VA
Printed in the United States of America.

FIRST PAPERBACK EDITION

Layout and Design Editor: Sarah Crossland

Library of Congress Control Number: 2015951246
Last Leaf Press, Charlottesville, VA

ISBN 978-0-9965708-0-0

To Susan at 60

Table of Contents

"If the world were merely seductive, that would be easy. If it were merely challenging, that would be no problem. But I arise in the morning torn between a desire to improve the world and a desire to enjoy the world. This makes it hard to plan the day."

—E.B. White

A Potentially Quite Remarkable Thursday

A Poem I Wrote in My Younger Days

A poem I wrote in my younger days
shows up on my desk right before dinner one night.
My god could that be you, the poem says,
grabbing me by both hands and giving me
the once over. *It sure as hell is*, I say,
grabbing the poem with both hands and giving it
the once over. We spend the rest of that night drinking
and reliving the old times, the dorm-room sex,
the cheap wine in one-bedroom flats,
the 2:00 am debates on the merits of Lennon
and whether Simon needed Garfunkel.

Five days later the poem is still hanging around
my kitchen table, making itself at home
and disturbing the poems of my present life
with tales of the old times, the dorm-room sex,
the cheap wine in one-bedroom flats,
the 2:00 am debates on the merits of Lennon, etc.

By this point I've grown tired of having to be
nice to this poem, but I can't figure out
a way to get rid of it without hurting its feelings.
Weeks later, I can hear it chattering away
in the back of a desk drawer, reliving the old times . . .

The One-Hit Wonder

He's still fanning the embers of a once-bright fire
in a bar or Legion hall near you, opening and closing with
the only song that made him any money, filling

the hour and 54 minutes in between with extended versions
of the nine other songs on the album that featured
the only song that made him any money, padding

the time in between those songs with bad covers
of Top 40 hits released in approximately the same year as
the only song that made him any money. That song

is all he's got, but it's one hit song more than any of the night's
93 paying customers can claim. Even now, its opening riff
is spinning the faithful back to a magical place and time,

just like it's spinning me—speeding by on the highway,
radio blaring, praying for the lightning strike that will make
a whole continent be-bop and sh-boom to one of my poems.

At Thirteen I Discovered
Art History

I can still picture my math teacher's
Rubenesque figure leaning against
the edge of her desk, one arm sweeping
gracefully toward the back of the room,
her head tilting up and slightly left
as she strains to hear what the bust
of the new girl is saying. As usual,
I'm distracted by the two dark-haired
odalisques whispering in front of me,
the early afternoon sun highlighting
the curve of their backs in a striking,
mid-nineteenth century French sort of way.
And though I also have trouble
keeping my eyes off the magnificent torso
of the neoclassical nymph poised
at the blackboard, her secrets kept
by a coy turn of the knee, I already suspect
that bookish guys like me are destined
to marry someone more like
the Impressionist girl in the first row,
the one with the demure smile
and simple black ribbon holding
the hair away from her ample
but enticingly vague bosom.

1:00-2:00 AM

The god who rules this hour is the god of flushing toilets, scampering mice, and distant radio tower lights. No longer having any ambition for advancement, he goes about his modest work with a philosophical outlook lacking in the God of Noon. Those feathery clouds that just blurred the full moon, for instance, don't particularly trouble him. He's a specialist in doubt and regret; his favorite music is whatever you listened to alone in high school. "Put on *The White Album*," he says as you settle in to reorganize your collection of unhealed wounds by descending order of date. He watches you work from a corner of the bed, singing the familiar words and occasionally interjecting a helpful observation. You're only half-finished when the hall clock chimes, and his voice fades like the whistle of a train you were too late to catch.

The Fire

We left at sunrise to repair the switchbacks
of the trail leading to the south ridge,
hard, sweaty work that made washing in the river
at day's end feel like getting a new body.
In the dinner line I asked the young ones

on each side of me where they were from
and what brought them to working the trails
for the summer, and they gave me respectful
answers before turning back to their plates.
At sunset everyone walked down to a fire

a few of them had made in a small clearing
in the birches and willows lining the riverbank.
A guitar came out and I laughed to hear one voice
and then four or five singing "Eleanor Rigby."
Ah, look at all the lonely people . . .

I said I could remember that song playing
on an AM radio station the year it came out,
which impressed them less than I'd hoped.
And so I settled back into a near perfect night
of cool canyon air and stars, red wine in cups

and talk of other people's dreams. The music
turned to songs my own son would know
and they began to dance, lean and graceful as cats,
hands touching, heads back, hands releasing.
I swayed unnoticed like one of the willow branches

caught in the fire's wind, until even that took
more effort than I cared to give. Back in my cabin
I fell into the restless sleep of the bone weary,
the fire's glow like a red star on the horizon,
my skin and hair still smelling of smoke.

Unchained Adolescent Melody

Fourteen and held to the world
by an AM station and the sputtering
flame of a bayberry candle I was
like a rock on those Saturday nights
alone in my room

                          no I was probably
more like an island   and oh
my very explicitly imagined love
        my darling
how I hungered for your touch
how I hungered

                how I hungered
for the touch of anyone
with fully developed breasts
because all I needed was
     love   love   love
yes love was all I needed   but oh
on those long lonely nights
with time going by so slowly
my cry-eye-eye-eye-ing
was all that touched
the sound of silence

Brown Mustard

They met at one of the three good restaurants
in their small college town, the star scholarship student
in his one sport coat and tie and the professor
with perfect diction who wouldn't be seen shopping
at the local A&P dressed in anything less.
They ordered hand-pressed Angus hamburgers
on homemade rolls and fell into flattering talk
of the professor's courses and the student's short list
of graduate schools. When their food arrived
the professor paused in mid-sentence to frown
at the ounce of yellow mustard in a porcelain cup
by the side of his plate. *Is there nothing else,*
he finally sighed to the waiter, *nothing grainy and brown?*
Later that night, huddled in the twin bed
of a candle-lit dorm room, the student told
the carpenter's daughter he would one day marry
how not having brown mustard was apparently
enough to ruin a fine restaurant hamburger.
They laughed long and easily that such a thing
could matter, but, of course, found in time
that it did.

History Lesson

My grandfather left school at fourteen
to work odd jobs until he was old enough
to join his Lithuanian kin chipping
anthracite out of the Pennsylvania hills.
Nine hours a day with five hundred feet
of rock over his head, then an hour's
ride home on the company bus
to a dinner of boiled cabbage and chicken.
When the second big war broke
he headed "sout," as he pronounced it,
for better work in the blast furnaces
churning out steel along the shores
of the Chesapeake. Thirty-two years
and half an index finger later he retired
to a brick rancher he built with his own hands
just outside the Baltimore city line.
The spring he got cancer and I got a BA
from a private college we stood under
a tree in his backyard while he copped
a smoke out of my grandmother's sight.
"Tell me, Pop," I said, wanting to strike up
a conversation, "how did you like
working in the mills all those years?"

He studied my neatly pressed white shirt,
took a long drag on his cigarette and spit a fleck
of tobacco near my shoes. *"Like,"* he said,
"didn't have a thing to do with it."

Air Conditioning

As a boy I'd have sacrificed my left nut
for the relief it could have bestowed
on those sweltering August nights
in our East Baltimore row house.
But cool inside air was forbidden fruit
in a neighborhood where the big sin
was thinking you were better than everyone else.
Furniture came from Montgomery Ward,
clothes and appliances from Sears.
Cars were Fords or Chevys. College was a place
to send boys too weak for the mills
and girls too smart or flat-chested to marry.
A secret committee of women in their forties
decided such matters over cigarettes
and coffee, then posted their decrees
on screen doors in a script only the wives
in their twenties knew how to read.
The year after my family set sail
for the suburbs, a window air conditioner
was approved in the hope it would keep
the disability checks of a committee member's
asthmatic mother-in-law coming.
When the old woman finally died,

the committee member and her husband
moved back into the bedroom they'd let her use,
arguably the best one in the house,
and who could complain about them
keeping the AC after the way they'd taken care
of his cantankerous mother for so long?
Over the next few years it turned out
every house in the neighborhood had
at least one elderly relative or maybe a baby
with some kind of respiratory problem.
No one's suffering, however, was bad enough
to need central air conditioning.

Jesus H. Christ

He was more of an invisible smoking buddy
to my father than a divine companion whose assistance
might occasionally be worth calling upon.
A pal who could appreciate the parade of clowns
cluttering the narrow streets of my father's life—
the bozos who rode his ass down the highway,
the neighbors who cut their grass on Sunday evening,
everyone who had anything to do with the drill
whose trigger broke the first time he used it.
Bosses. Hippies. *Jeeesus H. Christ.*
The name rolled out of his mouth like a wave,
the long sound of the first syllable
crashing into the rocky shore of the last.
One of the great mysteries of my childhood
was what the "H" stood for. My best friend
was Catholic, and he didn't know. I sure as hell
wasn't going to ask my father.

Revelations, Chapter 1

At three I laughed when I told
my mother how silly it was
that the word people said for

the bird that lives on farms
and doesn't fly the bird that clucks
and lays eggs *yes that bird*

that bird had the same word
people said for what we ate at dinner
with mashed potatoes and corn

my mother told me about bacon
and hamburger that night too
though I hadn't asked about them

oh how could people do things
like that

Way To Go

What mattered most on those makeshift diamonds
was how many players each team would have.
If only eight, the batting team had to supply the catcher.
With seven we'd do without a right fielder
and needed to decide whether fly balls hit there
should be counted as fouls or outs. Six players
meant not having a shortstop, five that the pitcher
would cover first base. At those numbers we played
with the softest ball in the bag and banned
aluminum bats. Ties always went to the runner,
four fouls were an out.

Punching our gloves as the sun raced toward dinner,
we sorted into teams and agreed on the rules
in two minutes or less. No parties of the first or second part,
no papers to initial or arm-around-your-shoulder
side deals. Nothing to review and get back to you on.
And when the skinny kid from down the street
flailed his way across the packed clay and crabgrass
to make a miraculous catch of your sinking line drive,
even you nodded and said *Geez, way to go, man.*

Schrödinger's Cat *

In the tenth-grade basement parties where we tried
our new selves on for size, I was the philosopher
intent on impressing the potential bearers of my children
with how well I understood the true nature of things,

I mean like, how do you know that what *I'm* seeing
as the color green is the same thing as what *you're* seeing
as the color green because, you know, like it could be
that what *I'm* seeing as the color green is actually

what *your* brain is seeing as the color blue,
and anyway, man, I mean like have you ever considered
there could like, you know, be like an entire universe
inside this potato chip? I once spent half an hour

explaining to a beautiful brown-haired girl how I thought
everyone at the party was you know, sort of like
this famous cat I'd read about which, after being
subjected to a possibly fatal event, simultaneously existed

in a quantum state of both aliveness and deadness
until it was actually observed. It was a remarkable insight
for someone still three years from taking Psych 101,
and I felt sure the girl was getting it until she asked me

what color the cat was and did I like, you know,
have any idea how old it was? Fortunately,
I was so overcome by a sudden sensation of aliveness
that I couldn't speak or roll my eyes.

* *The subject of a famous thought experiment created by German
physicist Erwin Schrödinger in the 1930s to illustrate a paradoxical
principle of quantum theory called the superposition of states.*

Sarge, 1970

Sarge watched the world disintegrate
from his chair in the dining room
of our suburban Cape Cod, what little bit
of light he had to shed on the matter
coming from the tip of a cigarette.
College boys pranced for the TV cameras
and spat on the uniform he'd just traded
for a civil service coat and tie; the wife
who'd dutifully tended the home fires
during his last tour overseas was
missing in action at a neighborhood bar.
At fifteen, all I cared about was loosening
his grip on the length of my hair.

Years after he died, my mother told me
he'd retired from the Army so he wouldn't
have to serve in Vietnam. It was an act
his words could have made either cowardly
or courageous. But he'd surrendered
his voice to bourbon and water, and I suffered
his silence to grow locks that unfurled
in the hot summer breeze like the flag
of a new and terrible army he couldn't
bring himself to enlist in or fight.

Who Was the Best Man at Your Wedding?

In high school there wasn't a back road
within 50 miles he and I didn't cruise
the length of in the late hours of a Friday night,
earnestly sorting out each other's lives
while listening to the music that still defines us,
or sometimes letting the songs alone
do that difficult work. Once we drove
all the way to Philadelphia, two states
and 100 miles distant, before either of us
said anything; then on the trip back our banter
made a row of fast-food counter girls laugh
until their manager strolled by to ask
whether he could be of any assistance.
A few nights one of us cried in the other's presence,
an act which in that age of hard men
should have forged a bond between us
as sacred and strong as if we'd clasped cut palms
to mingle blood. Neither of us had much use
for such rituals back then, but now
I'd have gladly taken up a knife and more
to keep our lives from coming to this—
my face only a speck in his rearview mirror,

his name the secret answer a credit card company
is waiting for me to type.

To My Father

At forty I could finally understand what
it was like for you back then, coming home

from your small desk job to a brittle wife
and four unruly boys. The TV blaring

and toys on the floor. The mortgage.
You perfected swift and unpredictable rage

as you later perfected slow pulls on cigarettes
and puttering in the yard. You were dead

by the time I was finally old enough
to understand what that was like for you.

When I see you now you're as I first remember—
tall and smiling in the distance, the faint glow

of a cigarette in your raised right hand,
waving at your boy to catch up.

Another Poem Featuring Moonlight

In this one I'm sitting on the edge
of my bed after the night's first dream,
listening to the creaks and moans
of a bitter February night,
thinking about the way the light
of the full moon seems to change
what it touches in the same way
that time changes what I remember—
softening the harsh boundaries
between form and shadow, not fading
or deepening the colors of the sunlit hours
so much as simplifying them.
On a night rattling with the winds
of what might have been I can't think
of a more fitting landscape in which to wander:
enough darkness to let ghosts rise up
and do their necessary roaming,
enough light for me to see them coming
and let them pass.

Complaint

Life is exhausting
it's taking up
all my time
these days
including
weekends
live, live, live
it's all I have
time for Christ
even when
I'm asleep
I'm living
but let me
tell you
I am not
some kind
of machine
I can't keep
this up
forever
and then
what

Warning from the Boss

Let's grab a beer after work, I say
to myself right before quitting time.
I suppose I could do that, I answer,
somewhat startled by my offer.
I immediately begin to worry; I never
ask myself out for a beer after work unless
something is up. And sure enough,
I'm no sooner seated at the bar than I say
*I can't help but wonder whether
something has been bothering me lately.*
I scratch my chin and lean forward.
What makes me think that, I respond,
doing my best to sound nonchalant.
Well, I continue, *I seem distracted
and edgy lately, and frankly, the quality
of my work has declined noticeably.*
Hmm, I say after an appropriate interval,
I really can't think of any explanation.
I glance at the TV and clutch my beer.
Look, I say in my most serious voice,
*I'll do what I can to help. But it's
important for the whole team to be giving
110% right now; there's no room for slackers.*

I study my reflection in the window.
Right, I finally say as I finish my beer.
Good then, I reply as I settle up the tab.
I shake my hand and turn toward home.
It's raining. While I walk I replay the conversation
in my mind and find myself getting more
and more agitated. *Just who the hell
do I think I am talking to me like that?*
Damn right, I exclaim, sauntering up
and putting an arm around my shoulder.
I have never appreciated me like I should.

Manifesto: The Overachiever Liberation Front

All devices for denying & otherwise subverting the PRESENT
moment are subject to *immediate* **ASSASSINATION.**
SEVER your tethers to gadgets / SILENCE the perpetual buzz
FREEDOM for your eyes / your ears / your HANDS

ABOLISH the **TYRANNY** of fanatical **MEASUREMENT**
   NO MORE how much did you pay
   NO MORE how much do you weigh
   NO pass / NO fail
   NO anything on a scale of 1 to 100
  PROCLAIM UNIVERSAL AMBIGUITY

   MANDATORY 10:00 am **GAZE OUT WINDOW**
   MANDATORY 2:00 pm consultation
     with **PILLOW**
   MANDATORY 9:00 pm invocation
   of whatever you hold **SACRED**
   MORE campfires under glorious sky!
   MORE poetry & CHEAP art!
   MORE naked / **MORE** rain on face!
   MORE DOGS of humble ancestry!
   Unconditional **AMNESTY** for all **WINE**
   detained in cellars!

1. **REFUSE to SYNCHRONIZE**
2. **DEMAND RESTORATION**
   of the *analog* **RAINBOW**
3. **PLEDGE** your **ALLEGIANCE** to
   IM-PERFECTION

The Last Perfect Day

It could very well be this one:
the sun once again stifling
an incendiary sneeze, no acned rocks
bumping into Earth as she waltzes
with Moon. All the generals and politicos
are at a wedding or high school
band concert. My doctor hasn't called
to give me my latest test results;
in fact, no one has called to give me
the latest news from anywhere.
Every car I pass on my long drive home
stays on its side of the center line.
After a late dinner, a lone beer
miraculously appears in the back
of my refrigerator. It generates
the precise amount of happiness needed
to hold the whole teetering world
in perfect balance, at least
for another minute or two.

Poem of a Man Who Wants to Be Dangerous

like Charles Bukowski

This is the poem I've been thinking about
writing for years, the one where I wake up
in whatever seedy motel room the tequila
drops me, no shirt, no socks, just me

sweating on the bed in my unzipped jeans,
and the first thing I do is feel around
the debris on the nightstand for a cigarette,
because this is also the poem where

I smoke cigarettes and start fights by tossing
out the "f" word, *"f" you, Bukowski*, I say
to a guy who shows up in the middle of this poem,
and *"f" all your nutty girlfriends, too*,

and it's very possible I do, because this is also
the poem where I'm intimate with three
different women on one day, or maybe it's one
woman three different times on the same day,

I'll figure that part out later because this is also
the poem in which I find myself pressed for time
when a woman who claims she's my wife
chases me into the final stanza, where I hole up

in a shed remarkably like the one in my backyard,
tools and cans of flammable liquid everywhere.
This poem finally comes to an end when
I sink to the floor and light my last cigarette.

Step Right This Way

Most people have a pretty good idea
of what he's doing but don't expect
him to be so nonchalant about it.
"I'm digging my own grave,"
he announces with a smile to anyone
who seems puzzled or curious.
"Just look at this workmanship,"
he says while taking a smoke break
sitting on the dirt mounded
neatly to one side of the opening.
He points to the straight sides,
the square corners, and the level
bottom which he carefully sweeps
clean of pebbles each night.
Now that he's almost finished
he admits to having second thoughts
about the whole enterprise.
He waves a six-pack at the passers-by
in the hope one of them will come
close enough to stumble in,
but so far, no such luck.

The Man Who Runs Short
of Brains

A man's wife says he's running short of brains and he sure as
hell better get some soon. He's agreeable to her suggestion
and walks into town to see what's available. Frankly, he's
disappointed with the selection; all the brains in his price
range are spongy, machine-made models of lower quality
than the brain he's running short of. Not wanting to go home
empty-handed, he looks for something else his wife might
appreciate. He settles on a fine pair of nearly-new hands
two sizes larger than his own. You can never go wrong with
an extra pair of hands, his father used to say, but the man's
wife isn't happy. What do you want me to do with these, she
screams, chasing the hands into the hall closet. They cower
there for several days, holding each other and quivering.
Eventually they work up the courage to climb onto the shelf,
where they befriend the penis the man brought home for his
last anniversary. It has an excellent plan for what they should
do next . . .

The Beeping Wife

A man wakes to the sound of his wife beeping in the kitchen. He dresses and takes his usual place for breakfast. Beep, she says as he eats his oatmeal, beep BEEP as he leaves for work. He arrives home that evening to find her beeping on a chair in the living room. The sound makes it difficult for him to follow his favorite shows on TV, so he retires to their bedroom to read. Eventually she joins him, beeping intermittently even after he's turned off the light. If I don't do something about this, he thinks, I'm going to be very tired in the morning. He reaches over and depresses one of her nipples with his right index finger. Beep, she says. He depresses the other nipple and then both nipples simultaneously, but the beeping continues unabated. After an extended period of trial and error during which his language becomes increasingly coarse, he remembers the correct procedure and executes it with precision. La la la, she says. Beep beep, he replies.

The Librarian

Waiting at a light in a small New England town,
I look to my left and catch a glimpse
of myself sipping a beer in the Blue Moose Café.
I'm a professor at the liberal arts college
just down the road, or maybe I own the used bookstore
next door. The woman with long brown hair
seated across from me is the high school librarian.
We're about to become lovers.

A few days later I drive past myself picking apples
on the organic fruit farm I've scratched out
of the Virginia foothills. The blonde woman
steadying the ladder is from somewhere in Scandinavia.
We raised five children in an old farmhouse
heated with wood that we cut and split ourselves.
I love the way she still occasionally pronounces
the letter "j" like it's a "y."

It's like this everyplace I go—hiking the canyons
out West, strolling the streets of Manhattan,
lying here next to you on a lazy Sunday morning.
Wherever I am, I just can't help bumping into myself
in the middle of living a wonderful life.

Even now, I love the way you're staring at me
over those tiny reading glasses
as I do my best to explain that honestly, dear,
you were that librarian.

My Perfect Life in Nots

I'm relaxing by the creek that runs
through the back of our property,
sipping a pleasant cabernet franc not made
from grapes I grew in my own vineyard.
The late afternoon sky is a beautiful
not-Mediterranean blue; the trickle
of the creek doesn't sound anything
like the ocean lapping against
a black-sand beach. I don't bother
glancing at my watch because I'm not
running late for a Hawaiian luau
or a camel ride through the desert.
Halfway through the third glass
of not-my-own wine I notice
a snapping turtle not moving
on the opposite bank of the creek.
He's nowhere close to the size
of the turtles that live in the Galapagos.
Still, it's not a sight Susan would want
to miss. I stroll back to our house,
which does not overlook an olive grove
and which we are not restoring
with the help of amusing villagers
who don't speak English very well.

Six Inches

One minute I'm meandering down
a country road on a magnificent fall day,
lost in thought, radio playing,
and the next minute I feel my wheels

on the loose gravel of the shoulder,
there's a deafening bang and I'm
climbing out of what's left of my car.
The cop who came to investigate

was pretty sure I'd been speeding
but settled for lecturing me about how lucky
I was to walk away from such a crash,
that I'd be dead if my car had hit the tree

just six inches further to the left.
Anyone could see that what he said was true,
but it also struck me as I stood there
watching his car flash red and blue

that it was equally true the accident
would not have happened at all
if a raging storm some sixty years ago
hadn't blown an acorn six inches closer

to the road than where it would've landed
on a day as sunny and calm as the one
we were in. It was a point I thought deserved
serious exploration—though perhaps

not just then, I decided, with a hundred birds
singing their tiny hearts out overhead
and the sky raining down yellow leaves,
and definitely not with the cop.

Passing Lives

At a late hour I pull up to the only open toll booth and stare at the woman working there. "Forgive me," I say after a moment, "but I just came to the point in the experience of my whole life passing before my eyes when I have a disturbing premonition of the catastrophic event that causes my whole life to pass before my eyes in the first place." She leans out of the booth and puts her hand on my arm. "I'm sure that's quite unsettling," she replies, "especially since at this point in the experience of your whole life passing before your eyes you can't be certain you're even going to survive the catastrophic event you've just had a disturbing premonition of." She has a warm, comforting voice; I can't help wishing I'd met her earlier in the experience of my whole life passing before my eyes. We chat for another minute or so, but unfortunately her shift isn't over until it's possibly too late.

Her Summer at the Lodge

She was a seasonal hire looking to spend
a few months in a place big enough to help her
find the trailhead for life's serious work;
even after six weeks, though, no one on her crew

could really claim they knew much about her.
Her roommate reported her missing when
she hadn't returned to their cabin by midnight.
Someone else remembered her saying she might

hike up the mountain after her shift ended.
By noon on that first day, the two local TV stations
were showing her college graduation picture
and clips of her mother and sister in Michigan

expressing the family's firm belief in a merciful God.
On the second day a college official recalled her
as a good student, friendly and well-liked.
The head of the search team described the terrain,

which even in June was often treacherous with ice
where the big firs kept the paths in shade all day.
Guests at the lodge could see her car, an old Toyota,
cordoned off at the far end of the main lot by the sign

for the trails. It sat crooked in the space a few feet
from the chain separating the gravel from the grass.
A blue jacket sprawled across the back seat
next to a water bottle and a state map she'd folded

to the lodge's location. By sundown on the third day
everyone was waiting for somebody else to say what
they all knew. It was of some consolation, though,
that no one was suggesting foul play.

Passing Time with the Scorpion Nun

During the long wait in the station
she tells me she is French and has lived
for three years in a Buddhist abbey
overlooking the sea in Nova Scotia.
Her eyes are blue and never still;
an old surgical scar snakes across
the back of her recently shaved head.
Her bare right shoulder bears
a small red tattoo—a spider?
No, a scorpion. She clutches
the white-bead mala used to count
mantras that remove obstacles.
Her face is oddly angular and carries
the pain of a poor complexion;
still, it seems to me a face
that some man might have loved.
We chat for a while about the weather
and the book I've been reading,
then fall into silence until her train
arrives and she takes her leave.
All these years later, I'm still not
the kind of man who could ask:
why a scorpion?

Memories of the Girl Who Works Thursday Mornings at Starbucks

She's of no more consequence to me
than any of the other people I brush
lightly against in the course of a week—
young, neither attractive nor unattractive,
appropriately attentive to my needs,
nothing in particular I can think of
that would explain the starring role
she played in the unruled hours
between midnight and dawn last night.
But as I stand in front of her now
in the bright light of a Thursday morning,
the memory of that performance
makes me blush when our hands touch
in the exchange of my usual fare;
she raises an eyebrow and appears puzzled
by the two five-dollar bills I cram
into the jar on the counter.

The Oracle

An almost entirely true story

The first time we met she took out
her journal and showed me a sketch
she'd made of a recurring dream—
a solitary, leafless tree standing beside
a dark stream flowing through
a field of tall, straw-colored grass.
She felt sure it was a place she had visited
and should be able to recognize.
"Of course it's a place you've visited
and should be able to recognize," I said
between bites of a sandwich, "It's your life."
She gasped and spilled her Coke.
"Think of yourself as the tree," I continued,
handing her a pile of napkins.
"You're standing fixed and dormant
in a nondescript landscape while
the great river of life, which isn't
much more than a creek in your case,
trickles slowly along beside you."
"That's fucking brilliant!" her boyfriend
Eddie said. She thought so, too,
and for the next few days followed me

everywhere I went, filling me in
on the most intimate details of her life,
pleading with me to tell her what
she should do next. "Christ," I finally said
after midnight on the fourth night,
"leave Eddie, quit your job, and move
to New York City." She stared intently at me
for several minutes, then walked away.
And that turned out to be the last time I saw her,
though I do still occasionally run into Eddie,
who continues to refer to me in a loud voice
as "The Great All-Seeing Oracle Shithead."

Free Tibet

Stopped in traffic I notice a sticker on the car
in front of me pleading for someone to *Free Tibet,*
and a picture of the Himalayas forms in my mind
and I think *yes, I know where Tibet is,* and *yes,*
I'd like Tibet to be free, though I can't say
I'm entirely sure what I can do to help it be free,
except, that is, for the always appropriate
gesture of sending money to the Tibetans
so they can buy the things they think might help
them become free, but before I can decide
how much would be a good amount to send
to the Tibetans I start thinking about
all the other places that could use my money
to buy freedom things—Africa, for instance,
or a country closer to home where they speak
Spanish and everyone is poor, which I'm pleased
with myself for seeing is a form of not being free,
and of course that leads me to America's cities,
which are filled with people who are poor
and can't go where they want because they might
get shot or the bus service to their neighborhoods
is crappy, and I wonder would all those poor American
city people appreciate the irony in me owning
not one but two cars yet being unable to go

anywhere while I'm thinking about them?
Then the traffic moves for a while and I'm happy,
until it slows again before the next exit
and I notice a sticker on the car in front of me
pleading for someone to *Support Our Troops*,
and a picture of a Marine forms in my mind
and I think *yes, I know some troops.*

The Alliance

My crazy neighbor Dave waves me to the road
by his house to see something he swears
I'll find *abso-fucking incredible.* And this time
he's right, for strewn there a few feet from the end
of a single set of skid marks are the intertwined
limbs and tails of a fox, a raccoon, and an opossum,
three most unlikely fellow travelers all in what
Dave has determined to be precisely the same condition
of deadness. For Dave, this is further evidence
of some kind of grand wildlife conspiracy, the purpose of which
he has not yet determined. Having no explanation
of my own to offer for the carnage in front us,
I nod and follow him back to his porch.
Over a cup of coffee we watch six buzzards
slowly spiral out of the sky and take up positions
around the previous night's casualties, which Dave
had the decency to line up on the shoulder of the road.
You know, those birds are just like the U. S. Marines,
he whispers to me as they begin their grim work,
they never leave a comrade behind.

National Security

Dave hit another deer last night, which he swears
was an intentional act on the part of the deer.
Dave knows this because the look in the deer's eyes
was the exact same look as what he's seen in the eyes
of those young Arabs on TV with bombs taped to their chests,
and, he asks me, have I ever noticed how it's always
the young impressionable deer taking on our cars
and trucks, never the *mullah deer* with their
big-ass antlers? Dave is convinced those big bucks
are the behind-the-scenes organizers of a campaign
to terrorize us members of the homo sapien race
into not leaving our houses so the various members
of the deer race can enjoy free and unfettered access
to our homo sapien azalea bushes and corn crops.
To Dave it's utterly ridiculous that you have to buy
a hunting license to put a bullet or an arrow
in such an animal. *Shoot first and ask questions later*
is his philosophy, only he can't think of even
one question a homo sapien could need to ask
about killing a deer. It's become, he declares
on his way to get a second estimate on his truck,
a matter of *national security.*

The Copperhead

I'm in the thick of the final line-by-line review
of my department's annual budget
when Susan calls with urgent news.
*There's a big copperhead snake coiled
right outside the front door*, she says,
and *YES, I am absolutely, 100% sure
that it's a GODDAMN COPPERHEAD.*
I exhale into the phone and take a moment
to consider her statement. When I answer,
it's in that unnaturally calm voice even I
sometimes find irritating. *Well*, the voice says,
*why don't you see if you can persuade it
to stay right where it is until I drive home?*
Silence. Then the sound of Susan inhaling,
and more silence. Eventually I hear
her equally calm voice saying *Never mind,
I'm sorry I bothered you.*

When I make it home at my usual hour
I find Susan relaxing with a novel in a chair
on the front porch. I look to her right
and instinctively jump back when I see it:
a thick-bodied, three-foot long *copperhead*.
She restrains a smile and without raising her gaze

motions with one finger toward a shovel
leaning against the house. I nod and begin
the delicate work of scooping up the snake,
one piece at a time.

To the Field Mice: My Final Terms

I am by most accounts a compassionate and even
generous man. Consider, if you will, our neighbors
the birds, whom I magnanimously provide
with food & housing in return for no more than
the promise of a song & fluttering dance.

Whereas you, with not so much as that to offer,
have shown (and I regret this is the word I must use)
the *audacity* to presume entitlement to winter residence
in the Main House, which is to say that structure occupied
by myself & family and maintained in accordance with
Generally Accepted Standards of Human Cleanliness
(excluding certain Adolescent Living Zones).

With the cold weather descending on us once more
and in consideration of my aforementioned compassion,
desire for peaceful coexistence, etc., etc., I herewith
present you the *Final Terms* under which I would find it
acceptable for you to maintain a presence in the Main House:

1. That you confine your nests & movements to the clearly
    marked Mouse Zones in the basement & attic, and *further*,
    that UNDER NO CIRCUMSTANCES shall you make

any appearance in the Human Zone, i.e. the entire area
of the Main House outside the designated Mouse Zones;

2. That you enter & exit said Mouse Zones solely through
   the several openings to be established & maintained
   exclusively for that purpose;

3. That you submit & adhere to a Waste Management Plan
   for the containment & disposal of fecal matter,
   such plan to be approved solely by *Myself*;

4. That you maintain your population at the level to be
   negotiated & incorporated into this agreement,
   subject to verification via random inspections
   of the Nesting Districts in the Mouse Zones.

Though I most earnestly hope you will see
the reasonableness of these Terms, I would be remiss
if I did not also advise you I am prepared to secure
the Main House with individually triggered
border protection devices (ITBPDs). Further,
I have acquired certain other means of mass destruction
to be deployed in the event all other efforts
to reach an accommodation fail. Should you doubt
my resolve to use said means of destruction,
I direct you to the termites, if you can find one.

The Angel Apologizes, Profusely

Let me begin by saying it had become impossible
to get their attention in the usual manner.
They were never alone; they chattered to the air

constantly. If I hovered over them in flaming robes
they'd say "hmmm, nice special effect" and turn
right back to their gadgets. If I sent them Mary's face

on a pancake I'd find it on eBay within a week.
Who needs divine visitations with all the prophecy
and gnashing of teeth available on cable news?

So perhaps I was a tad bit desperate the night
a couple of Cherubim said why not whip up
a flood, a really big one, *that* will get them going,

but I said no you'd made some sort of pact
with them on that, ABSOLUTELY NO FLOODS,
and then I thought what about something

celestial, a close encounter with an asteroid,
or maybe a comet, just a small one—
why they've even made several movies about it,

they'll be holding candles and singing Kumbaya
in front of the United Nations for weeks—
and well, yes in hindsight I can appreciate that

"close" and "small" are rather imprecise terms
and yes I certainly do have much to learn
about the physics of gravitational attraction,

but notwithstanding all that let me say
I know how fond you were of them
and I am truly, *truly* sorry.

A Potentially Quite Remarkable Thursday

I awoke this morning at the usual time
and in the usual manner. No midnight
call from the Dalai Lama urging me
to fulfill my special purpose to humanity,
no disheveled starlet banging on my door
and shamelessly begging me to please
take her back. Over my usual breakfast
I confirm I did nothing in the previous day
worth analyzing on the morning TV shows.
I do, however, note with some satisfaction
my continued absence from the obituary section
of the local newspaper. It inspires me
to shave and put on a respectable shirt
before the mail lady arrives at 2:00 pm;
I have a distinct feeling this could be the day
I am officially notified of my possible selection
to receive a major prize.

Keynote Speech

And to show us how we can all Unleash the Power Within,
the distinguished speaker would like everyone to stand.
Everyone stands. Next, he would like everyone to crouch
down and jump. Thousands of eyes look left and right; the
Gold Circle Award winners crouch down and jump, followed
by clumps of everyone else. The speaker is pleased. In fact,
we've done so well he would like us to jump again. Everyone
jumps again, this time in unison. The speaker is very pleased.
He walks to the edge of the stage and leans forward to ask us
something. *Do we have any idea*, he says, *of how small we are
in relation to the earth, with its vast continents and oceans*?
Thousands of feet shuffle. It's a puzzling question; even the
Gold Circle Award winners know they are small in relation
to the earth. Well, the speaker triumphantly informs us with
a broad grin, each of us has just overcome the gravitational
force of the entire earth twice in the past minute! We give
ourselves a vigorous round of congratulatory applause. No
one sits, however, until the speaker says please, everyone, take
your seats.

Flying Lessons

I'm sipping a cup of coffee on the back porch
watching a fly land on my left wrist.
Each time I begin a lazy swat with my right hand
it makes a figure-eight over to the railing
and then returns to the exact same square inch
of skin by my watch. We do this over and over again—
lazy swat, figure-eight to railing, land on wrist.
I'm not sure why this particular fly wants to spend
a measurable part of its twenty-some day flyhood
sitting on my arm, but its persistence impresses me.
When, I think, was the last time I showed similar
determination in the face of even modest adversity?
I'm still working up an answer when the fly
abandons me for a new enterprise involving
something I can't quite make out in the grass—
a turd, perhaps, or the desiccated carcass of a mouse.
It wastes no time dwelling on the success or failure
of the recently ended Mission of the Wrist.
That, too, strikes me as worthy of mention,
even admiration.

Creek View

I rest in the unmowed grass by the creek
on a cool May morning, lulled nearly to sleep
by a rose-scented breeze and the murmur
of water pardoning its way past smooth stones.
Somewhere not so far from this little valley
accomplished men with three-sport sons
make banks and governments hum;
someone's skilled hands stitch damaged hearts
or summon a symphony from brass and wood.
Somewhere rows of stern-faced men
stand ready to do the unspeakable deeds
that will keep me safe for one more day.
I praise them. I praise everyone with the will
to do the world's work while I dawdle
by this creek thinking up poems to write,
mostly about myself—this one, for instance,
which I've decided to end by likening
myself to a physician who in his old age
comes to see that the sacred oath he swore,
the one about first doing no harm,
begins with his own soul.

The Neighbors from the City

I walk down to the new neighbors' house
and knock on their door. After a brief exchange
of pleasantries, I tell them that ten or fifteen
of their hens have wandered across
the driveway we share and into my meadow.
"It's not that I mind," I hasten to add,
"but they're going to be easy pickings
for the hawks and other predators that live
in this neck of the woods." The wife,
a slender woman with a corner-office voice
and silk for skin, laughs and touches my arm
as she says she supposes her husband
will just have to hire someone to put up
a proper pen then. Neither she nor the husband
mention any plans to sell or share
their abundance of eggs, and when the time comes
to take my leave, I don't bother repeating
the point I stopped by to make.

Vines

They're everywhere the sun shines
for an hour or two—bittersweet strangling
the straight trunks of the ashes and oaks,
grapevines snaking through the low limbs
of the dogwoods and cherries, honeysuckle
winning the battle for the forest's edge
against even the wild roses and blackberries.
Take a spring nap in the tearthumb
by the creek and what's left of you
won't be found until after the first frost.

I can't count the hours I've spent cutting,
tugging, and dragging long tangles of vines
from the many places I've decided
they don't belong. Even on days I wore
a canvas coat I'd come back to the house
at twilight with my forearms bruised
and covered in scratches. More than once
on those nights I woke from a restless sleep
to find that I'd been dreaming of vines;
my calloused hands ached to touch you then,
but I was too afraid I'd cut you into pieces
or never let you go.

The Insomniac

What he knows of his neighbors he knows
from their lights, and lately he's noted
a number of reasons for concern. The old man
across the street has gone from peeing
three times each night to four, and the new baby
in the house on the corner appears to have colic.
In a troubling development, the middle-aged couple
in the blue house next to the baby house
has been sleeping in separate bedrooms
for more than a month now, much longer
than he would expect for a marital argument
or a case of the flu. On a happier note,
the young couple to the left of them has started
going to bed at the same time most nights
during the week instead of just on Saturdays,
and they're in the same second-floor room
whose curtained glow is barely visible
from his own darkened perch. Two people
have recently switched from taking early-morning
showers to lingering in late-night baths,
a change that he finds interesting, but probably
not of great consequence.

A Disturbing Development

Under cover of darkness a nicely-branched,
seven-foot-tall beech tree managed
to sneak onto my property last night
and plant itself in the grove of maples and oaks
along the north side of my front meadow.
I was home all night and didn't see or hear
anything suspicious, yet there it was this morning,
waving a hundred yellow fingers at me
barely an arm's length off the path I've walked
twice a day nearly every day for twenty years.
I don't have any particular objection to this beech tree
taking up residence there, but its presence
on this fall morning still troubles me:
what else has been going on in my woods
that I should know about?

Death of a Cardinal

From a distance he's no more
than a pinprick on winter's
milk-white skin, a small wound
easily healed. One wing
flutters as I draw near;
the long feathers of his tail
flex twice and then are still.
In the warm nest of my hand
he trics to stand but soon
settles with his head tucked
tight against my thumb.
I stroke the feathers of his breast
and return him to the snow
with an apology for thinking
about how I will begin
this poem.

The Perfect Metaphor for My Life

It comes to me late one night while I'm driving down the
interstate at 55, sipping a Diet Coke and listening to songs
from my youth. I'm in the middle lane, maintaining a safe
distance from the cars in front of me, keeping close watch
in the rearview mirror for anyone who might overtake me
from behind. Though there's not much traffic I still signal my
intention to change lanes well in advance. On this particular
night, I'm so enamored with having come up with the perfect
metaphor for my life that I forget to get off at my exit. Trying
to find my way along the dark, honeysuckle-scented back
roads, the moon hanging over a small town on the horizon—
for the first few miles, it's exciting.

The Good Citizen

Through no fault of my own I woke up
nearly sixty years old this morning.
No special consideration for paying
my mortgage on time, no rebates
for all the years of recycling and laughing
at other people's bad jokes.
Nothing for writing poetry and voting
Democratic in every election.
Over my morning bowl of Cheerios
I believe I worked out
where this is going to end up, yet—
how could such a thing
be possible?

On Finding My Mother Dead

You who screamed me into this world
at 3:43 am on a military hospital bed
are dead

you who packed my lunches and one time
took me shopping without any of my brothers
are dead

washer of my dirty clothes and snotty noses
you are dead

maker and breaker of holiday feasts
you are dead

merciless keeper of the family accounts
you are dead

you are dead on your bed
one arm arced gracefully over your head
you are dead

and no one sang you to sleep
you are dead
and no one can sing you awake

(you are dead)

Canyon Letter to Andy

The truth is things got to where I felt like I could hardly
keep up anymore. The world seemed speedy
and past my reach; everyone I met was on life support
from a gadget I didn't own and couldn't make
any sense of. My life had turned soft, like my hands,
soft and small and suited to fine work.

So at dawn yesterday I put some food and a down bag
into a pack and I drove out the old Forest Service road
to a canyon trail no one's used in years. I left my compass
in the car, which was foolish, and started picking my way
down the loose rock of the east rim. I resolved to walk
until I came to a place quiet enough for me to find out

if I could still hear myself, not knowing whether I'd be
more afraid if I could or I couldn't. I camped against
the canyon's steep west wall, near where the stream pulls
close to the ponderosas. It was a fitful night, too,
cold and loud with the sound of the coyotes,
but I've spent more than a few worse and for less cause.

This morning I gave some thought to just staying there,
making my end like an Indian warrior who walks deep
into the woods and lays himself under a tree when

he decides it's a good day to die. After a time, though,
I came to see what I'm guessing you've known for a while,
that every day is a good day to die, and to live.

Not being sure how the trip back up the face might go,
I decided to write you this letter in the hope you'd know
I'd learned something important before my feet slipped
off the trail. And if it turned out they didn't slip, I figured
I'd deliver this to you with my own hands, still as small
as when I left but a little more ready for the work ahead.

On Being Remembered

The threshold is exceptionally high.
Even Hitler is becoming small;
soon only the jackboots
and funny mustache will be left.
Shakespeare may linger,
but only until we all speak Machine.
Nixon is already a footnote,
Reagan a stamp. My great grandparents
are three pictures and a handful
of anecdotes that might be true.
My parents fit in a shoebox
which my great grandchildren
will vaporize before they delete me
from the digital cloud where they live.
Even so, I take time this morning
to cut the vines I see tugging
down a sapling. Even so, I take time
to leave you this poem.

The Buddhist Master Instructs Me on Life and Death

After meditating with him
for a month I ask what happens
when we die and

he tells me he doesn't know
and I say but you are
a great master of the dharma

yes he replies but not
a dead one

Some Advice for Clearing Brush

Walk noisily to declare your presence.
The rabbits and deer will leave
as soon as they hear you coming,
but the snakes need time
to process your intentions.

Take a moment to be certain
of what you're cutting.
Many stems look alike
down close to the ground,
especially when they're young.
Look up occasionally.

Don't begrudge the wild roses
for whipping thorns across
your face and arms,
or the honeysuckle
for tangling your feet
and pulling the pruners
from your hands. You'd do
the same in their place.
Honor them with a clean cut.

Never begin when you're angry
or you might not stop
until there's nothing left
to hold the soil.

Always wear gloves
and keep your eye
on the blade.

What the Old Man Wants the Young Nurse to Know

Everything he tells her has something to do with *time*,

That despite what everyone said it didn't heal all his wounds,
it only gave him the chance to make friends with his pain;

That it did go by quickly, that he remembers shipping off
to Korea like it was yesterday and now here he is;

That in hindsight he wasted as much of it hoping for things
that never came to pass as he did regretting the things that did;

That if he's truthful, not having enough of it wasn't the reason
he didn't accomplish everything he wanted to in life;

That everybody he knows who waited for the perfect time
to get married or apologize ended up watching TV alone;

That all the busy bees who say time is money are in for
a big surprise when they run out of it, just like he has;

That though you can count the years he has left on one hand,
he's already outlived both his parents, god rest their souls;

That he always made a point of being on time, and even
the people who didn't like him had to give him that much;

That he doesn't mind if his doctor is running late this morning
because, frankly, the news hasn't been very good recently.

Susan at 60

A few days after New Year's I found
the juniper fire she'd made in the woods
to burn away the bad energy lingering
from the year her parents' bodies failed them,
a year of waiting rooms and phone calls,
medical forms and day-long car rides.
It was important, she said, to pass
through the smoke seven times, circling
the flames in a clockwise direction.
My mind of cross-checked rows
and columns is never going to understand
how that works. Yet hers moves easily
through a world that requires no proof,
where each month's moon is called by its name
and a little speck of magic hums
inside every river stone and animal bone.

Eagles, she tells me, are for people who love
mirrors. Her spirit guide is the vulture,
graced with a difficult beauty,
expecting nothing in return for its unglamorous
but highly useful work.

The Flood

Four times in our years on that land
the creek below us raged out of its banks,
tugging down old walnuts and oaks,
burying the trails I'd labored so long to make
in a thick layer of silt and debris.
The last time, in late August of the year
we decided to leave that place,
we scrambled down the rain-slicked hill
as night fell and stood giddy and afraid
while the water churned in front of us.
Somewhere in the distance we heard a tree
snap. In the last light the water
rose up over our boots, and for one
exhilarating instant we weren't sure
which way we should step.

In Gravity's Defense

Light, we have praised you too much
for your graceful dance from moon
to steamy summer meadow,
your playful conversation

with waterfall and autumn leaves,
the way you peek through
the strands of a woman's hair
and caress bare skin

with the softest of touches.
When you blind us we recoil
as in the presence of truth revealed;
we are abject when you leave us.

For your unglamorous sister
who holds the mirror of the moon
in place and makes the water fall,
no songs are sung, no glasses raised.

Forgive, then, her small pleasure
in pulling down the perky breast,
her satisfaction in passing sentence
on every missed step,

her accountant-like insistence
that rules are rules
and everything must
fall into place.

The Last Leaf

By the end of October it was the only leaf
left on the big branch overhanging the end
of the driveway, a conspicuous speck of yellow
flapping *have a nice day* as I left for work
all through the meager days of November
and December, and *welcome home,*
how very good to see you as I turned back
into the driveway after a tiring day,
and what else could I do in the face
of such persistent cheerfulness except
give a friendly wave back and say *yes,*
how very nice it is to see you, too—
so that is just what I did every morning
and every evening alone in my car,
until the day in early March when the leaf
was no longer there. Yet all these years later,
when I close my eyes and remember
the months of numbness after the Towers fell,
the world spiraling into hatred and war,
it's that one tattered leaf I see, so stubbornly
and utterly in love with *up.*

The Year Everything Seemed to Work Out

A team of Navy Seals snuffed bin Laden
and no more towers fell. The economy
healed itself while the politicians yelled
about harmless things. Our daughter
married an honorable man, our son
moved out. Your father died, peaceably.
We drove west singing Beatles tunes,
and camped in canyons next to Indian ruins.
A wood duck finally nested in the box
I'd nailed to the big oak down by the creek.
The billions of cells in our bodies
went quietly about their business, making
just enough of this and not too much of that.
No signs of rebellion anywhere,
even our knees.

A Good Year for Walnuts

Fifty-some years in the company of trees
and I still can't say what makes a good year
for walnuts, though surely this will be one;
a week left in September and the first few
are already on the ground. A short séance
with a gadget screen and the ether would
no doubt tap a hundred answers back to me,
but on this morning I do the math and decide
I still have enough seasons left to come up with
an answer of my own. It will be exciting work, too,
recording the vagaries of the spring rains
and summer sun, chronicling frost dates
and dew points, correlating quantities
and weights of walnuts and acorns.
I pause outside the barn and imagine
the banquet where I'm ready to announce
my findings: a family gathering in autumn,
Thanksgiving perhaps, when the years
have pushed me to the head of the table.
Our children exchange uneasy glances
and touch their spouses' hands as I clear
my throat to begin. The spouses shush
our grandchildren and look at me with thin smiles
on tilted heads. I tell everyone I will endeavor

to be brief, but this is, after all, a topic
of considerable importance. I speak convincingly
of weather patterns and pollinators, weave in
a few amusing asides on the habits of squirrels.
I conclude by modestly thanking you,
my faithful research assistant and baker
of dozens of black walnut pound cakes
in the name of science, the person without whom
I assure the assemblage none of this
would have been possible. You smile
and ask whether anyone would like seconds.

Acknowledgements

These poems first appeared in the following print or online journals, some in slightly different versions:

Allegro Poetry Magazine: "Jesus H. Christ" and "The Buddhist Master Instructs Me on Life and Death"

Asinine Poetry: "Warning from the Boss" and "The Beeping Wife"

The Connecticut River Review: "Free Tibet"

Every Day Poets: "Complaint" and "Unchained Adolescent Melody"

Hobart: "Way to Go"

Moon City Review: "1:00-2:00 AM"

Passager: "Canyon Letter to Andy" and "In Gravity's Defense"

Poemeleon: "Sarge, 1970" and "Manifesto: The Overachiever Liberation Front"

Poetry Quarterly: "A Potentially Quite Remarkable Thursday"

The Poet's Domain: "A Poem I Wrote in My Younger Days," "Poem of a Man Who Wants to Be Dangerous," and "The Angel Apologizes, Profusely"

River Poets Journal: "The Librarian"

The Sow's Ear Poetry Review: "A Good Year for Walnuts"

The poem "Who Was the Best Man at Your Wedding?" appeared in the anthology *Objects in the Rear View Mirror*.

68258938R00063